How to Spot a Dangerous Man
Workbook

≈ *About the Author* ≈

Sandra L. Brown holds a master's degree in counseling. She is the founder and former executive director of Bridgework, Inc., a multifaceted nonprofit center for victims of violent crime. There, she provided both administrative leadership and clinical service through individual and group counseling.

She has worked as a therapist at hospital inpatient programs, residential treatment facilities, intensive outpatient programs, and other nonprofit treatment programs. She has been a keynote speaker, conference teacher, and workshop and retreat leader. She has taught counseling courses at the college level.

Sandra has provided consulting for human-service agencies in the area of program development for trauma-related disorders. She has assisted in international program development for the abandoned street children in Rio De Janeiro, Brazil. She is a frequent guest of radio call-in shows and has hosted and produced her own TV show, *A Voice for Victims*.

She is the author of the books *Counseling Victims of Violence* and *The Moody Pews*, as well as numerous articles on clinical counseling and personal-growth issues.

Dedication

This book is dedicated to the women who shared with me
their stories about relationships with dangerous men. They did so
to help other women be safer.

It's also dedicated to my husband, Ken, who has shared with me
his insights on this topic, and to my girls, Lindsay and Lauren, that they may
enjoy meaningful, safe, and healthy relationships. And to Hunter House
Publishers and Kelley Blewster for their work on the book. And lastly to my
gal pals "The Ya Yas"— you keep me centered and supply me with
endless feedback about the world we live in!

Ordering

Trade bookstores in the U.S. and Canada please contact:

Publishers Group West
1700 Fourth Street, Berkeley CA 94710
Phone: (800) 788-3123   Fax: (800) 351-5073

Hunter House books are available at bulk discounts for textbook
course adoptions; to qualifying community, health-care, and govern-
ment organizations; and for special promotions and fund-raising. For
details please contact:

Special Sales Department
Hunter House Inc., PO Box 2914
Alameda CA 94501-0914
Phone: (510) 865-5282   Fax: (510) 865-4295
E-mail: ordering@hunterhouse.com

Individuals can order our books from most bookstores, by calling
(800) 266-5592, or from our website at **www.hunterhouse.com**

How to spot a dangerous man

a dangerous man Workbook

A Survival Guide for Women

Sandra L. Brown, M.A.

Hunter House
PUBLISHERS

Hunter House Inc., Publishers
PO Box 2914
Alameda CA 94501-0914

Project Credits

Cover Design: Brian Dittmar Graphic Design
Book Production: Jinni Fontana Graphic Design
Copy Editor: Kelley Blewster
Proofreader: Hunter House
Acquisitions Editor: Jeanne Brondino
Editor: Alexandra Mummery
Editorial Intern: Herman Leung
Publishing Assistant: Antonia T. Lee
Publicist: Jillian Steinberger
Foreign Rights Coordinator: Elisabeth Wohofsky
Customer Service Manager: Christina Sverdrup
Order Fulfillment: Washul Lakdhon
Administrator: Theresa Nelson
Computer Support: Peter Eichelberger
Publisher: Kiran S. Rana

Manufactured in the United States of America

8 7 6 5 4 3   Second Edition   10 11 12 13 14

Contents

Introduction 1

PART ONE | ASSESSING YOUR RISK LEVEL 7

Categories of Dangerous Men 8

Mythical Assumptions 11

Universal Red Flags 13

Family Traditions and Early Conditioning 17

Loopholes 21

Am I in Danger of Dating More Dangerous Men? 28

PART TWO | YOUR PAST EXPERIENCES WITH DANGEROUS MEN 31

Identifying Feelings 32

My First Dangerous-Man Experience 33

My Second Dangerous-Man Experience 45

My Third Dangerous-Man Experience 55

Part Two Summary 64

PART THREE | MAKING NEW CHOICES 65

Introduction to Part Three 66

Another Look at My First Dangerous-Man Experience 68

Another Look at My Second Dangerous-Man Experience 72

Another Look at My Third Dangerous-Man Experience 75

My Personalized Do-Not-Date List 78

Red Flags and Patterns in My New Relationships 80

Part Three Summary 83

In Closing 85

Resources 86

 # introduction

*The process out of which a person emerges is essentially an
inward process*

— IRA PROGOFF

(Note: This workbook was created as a supplement to the book
How to Spot a Dangerous Man Before You Get Involved *(Hunter
House, 2005). The workbook is not meant to stand on its own. The
main book examines in detail what makes men dangerous, the
nature of pathology as it relates to dangerous men, the various types
of dangerous men, and women's patterns in selecting dangerous
men as dating partners. The background information presented in
the main book is essential to understanding the concepts and questions presented in this workbook. To get the best results from doing
the exercises in this workbook, please familiarize yourself with the
material in the main book before beginning these exercises.)*

Dangerous men come in all sorts of packages, from all types of
backgrounds and families, from all lines of work. It behooves
women to understand this because we remain unsafe if we categorize dangerous men simply as people we "would not be attracted to." The reality is that at some time in their lives most
women have dated a type of man this book would categorize as
dangerous.

I define a *dangerous man* as any man who hurts a woman
emotionally, physically, sexually, spiritually, or financially. Dangerous men have wreaked havoc and caused pain in many women's
lives. For many of us, it took significant time to heal from the experiences. We may or may not have learned from them. We may
have failed to gain enough information and lessons from our experiences with dangerous men to keep us from repeating the pattern with yet another dangerous man. It is not uncommon for
women to date as many as four or five dangerous men before
they figure out their own personal patterns and respond by

choosing differently the next time. But in the meantime, each painful experience with a dangerous man leaves its emotional mark on a woman's life. And perhaps worse, each painful experience with a dangerous man unfortunately sets a woman up to date more dangerous men if she fails to recognize her specific patterns and stop the cycle of choosing dangerously.

This workbook is about inspecting your past and present relationships so that you can learn every possible insight from them. It will help you examine the type of men you have chosen and why you have chosen them. It will guide you in developing a personalized "do-not-date" list, compiled from an analysis of your past mistakes. You will write about your history using your own words. Thus, your do-not-date list becomes a reflection of your own experiences, selections, and insights.

≈ *Developing an Accountability Partner* ≈

When a tree grows by itself, it spreads out but does not grow tall. When trees grow together in the forest they help push each other up towards the sun.

— ANCIENT ASIAN PROVERB

I believe in the power of two or more. We seem to do better when we are paired up. That's why we date, marry, or have friends—because having others to do things with comforts and empowers us. In fact, I would go so far as to say that we do not heal in isolation; we heal in community.

Professionals in the field of psychology have long known that group therapy is often more effective than individual counseling. When someone is doing poorly in individual counseling because they are isolated, they often find their own voice, heal faster, and develop support systems for their ongoing recovery if we put them in group therapy. Some people have more success in their attempts to stop smoking, lose weight, or go back to school if they pair up with someone else who is aiming for the same goal. Together they can jump hurdles they might not have dared to on their own. A certain synergy happens when people who are on the same page in life motivate each other toward achieving their mutual goals.

Women who have experienced the same dangerous relationship patterns that we have often share our need to make better choices. As a part of healing from your past dangerous relationships and making new choices for the future, I suggest that you find a woman friend who also wants to change her unhealthy relationship patterns. Suggest to her that the two of you work through this workbook together. Plan to meet every week or two to share with each other the insights you have gained from reading the main book and your responses to the exercises in this workbook. Connecting regularly with another person who will help you examine your relationship choices as you help her examine hers is a great way of developing a support system. Think of this person as your "accountability partner."

Accountability partners can help you look at your past relationships. They can help you sort out your patterns and can support you in your efforts to develop a do-not-date list. Beyond that, they will point it out to you if they see you slipping or violating your do-not-date list and your values. Likewise, you will do the same for your accountability partner. You will invest in her desire for better relationships by helping, supporting, and, if necessary, even confronting her.

Accountability partners are honest with each other. They share information about their past and their current lives. They ask for input and give input. They confront each other for safety, and they keep communicating with each other throughout the processes of dating and making new choices. They let each other in on their thoughts, behaviors, and feelings, and they commit to each other not only to work through the workbook together, but also to begin living in concert with their respective do-not-date lists, in full view of each other.

Please give some thought as to who your accountability partner can be and how you will go about inviting her to change her choices and, ultimately, her life. With the power of two, you each face a potential future of healthier and safer relationships.

≋ *How to Use This Workbook* ≋

It is costly wisdom that is brought by experience.

— ROGER ASCHAM

A woman's ability to choose differently is only limited by the type of information she is given about what comprises a good or a bad choice. This workbook is designed to help you study and learn from your patterns of selecting, dating, and having relationships with dangerous men. It is formatted to reveal destructive choices you've made that have led to dangerous situations. How much you learn from and how much you get out of the exercises have a lot to do with the effort you put into them.

People often think it is sufficient to complete the exercises by merely reading through them and answering the questions mentally. But I encourage you to write down your answers to *every* exercise. Research has indicated that people learn as they write. They think more deeply, and more answers come as they engage in the process of writing. In addition, written responses can be reread days, weeks, or months down the road and may cause you to remember something that finally puts all the pieces together for you. A new answer to a question or a new insight may also emerge as you refresh your memory by reviewing your original answers.

As you complete the exercises, it is important to be open to what you find out about yourself. This is an insight-oriented process. It is not meant to shame you for making relationship mistakes or choosing dangerously. The book and workbook were developed for your growth. The more open you are to learning about yourself, the more you will receive from the exercises that you can use to change your life. Unlike completing the exercises in this workbook, gathering insight is not something you can do in a short period of time. Still, the workbook should help you in the longer-term process of acquiring wisdom. If you suspect that you are at risk for dating dangerous men, and if you confirm this after doing some of the exercises in this book, then you should remove yourself from the dating/marrying game until you've worked with a professional therapist. This workbook should provide some insight into whether or not you need the assistance of a professional counselor, but it is not a replacement for counseling. If you need it, get it. And stay out of relationships until you know for sure that you are able to choose differently.

Your friends and family members may have insights about the relationships you've had with dangerous men. While it is often painful to hear what others think, if you are truly trying to change your patterns, it may be worth hearing. Sometimes others remember things you have forgotten or see a situation in a different way that can help you to put things in perspective and understand how and why you got involved with the men you did. Consider asking trusted friends and family members for any thoughts they may have about your history with dangerous men.

The workbook is divided into the following three parts:

PART ONE ◈ *Assessing Your Risk Level*

Part One can be thought of as an introductory section because it reviews some key concepts from *How to Spot a Dangerous Man Before You Get Involved*. It includes descriptions of the eight categories of dangerous men, and it reshapes other material from the main book into questionnaires. It also goes into detail about the topic of loopholes: things women tell themselves to justify staying in unhealthy relationships. It asks you to identify loopholes you have used to talk yourself into staying in relationships with dangerous men.

Determining your risk level for continuing to get involved with dangerous men is important in helping you decide what kinds of intervention you might need. When all the information from the Part One questionnaires is considered, it can provide you with a deeper understanding of the ways in which you might be at risk for dating more dangerous men.

PART TWO ◈ *Your Past Experiences with Dangerous Men*

Part Two is where you will begin to examine your history with dangerous men. It is crucial that women develop a personalized language for spotting and avoiding dangerous men based on their own experiences. These exercises will help you to do that. You will be asked to recall childhood associations with men that may have contributed to your later dating choices, and you will identify patterns from your relationships with dangerous men. You will be given an opportunity to reconnect with the red flags you've ignored in the past. The good news is you can still learn their lessons, even today.

PART THREE ◆ *Making New Choices*

Here you will put all the pieces together from the work you did in Parts One and Two. You will start by looking once again at your past relationships with dangerous men. You will identify what you learned from them, and for each man you will compile a list of characteristics that qualify him as dangerous. From these lists you will create your personalized do-not-date list. You can think of your do-not-date list as your higher conscience, your personal line in the sand, your special code for judging a relationship's safety. Honoring it will bring you much closer to avoiding dangerous men.

Part Three also contains a worksheet that asks you to write about what is happening in your current relationship. It asks you to compare your current partner's characteristics to your do-not-date list. Here is where you can begin to practice what you have learned. If you're not currently involved with anyone, keep this questionnaire handy so you can work through it the next time you consider dating someone.

There are three copies of each of the exercises that have to do with your past relationships, allowing you to write about your experiences with up to three dangerous men. *If you've dated more than three dangerous men, make enough photocopies of all the relevant exercises in Parts Two and Three to allow you to complete them for every dangerous man you've been involved with.* Don't make the mistake of minimizing a relationship with a dangerous man on the grounds that you "never got too serious with him." That relationship is still an important part of your dating history because it holds clues to your patterns, and learning from those clues is key to changing your future."

My hope for you as you complete the workbook is that you develop not only *insight* but also the ability to take the necessary *action* to lead you away from dangerous men and toward healthier and safer choices.

PART ONE

Assessing Your Risk Level

Categories of Dangerous Men

There is, in their tone, a dangerous gentleness—so much gentleness that the safe reserve of their soul is broken.

— D.H. Lawrence

From my years of working with dangerous men and the women who get involved with them, I have concluded that dangerous men generally fall into the following eight categories. For an in-depth look at each of these groups, see Chapters 3 through 10 in *How to Spot a Dangerous Man Before You Get Involved*.

THE PERMANENT CLINGER ◆ He is a needy, victim-based man who will give a woman a lot of attention in return for all his needs being met all the time. He fears rejection above all else, so he is jealous of other people in your life. He will ask you to give up your outside life and make your world revolve around him. He will try to convince you that he has been wounded and that you can "heal him with your love" if you will focus only on him. He may threaten to be "wounded forever" if you don't do as he asks, or he may use guilt to try to keep you in a relationship you no longer want to be in. Women have the overwhelming sensation of "having the life sucked out of them" by these men.

THE PARENTAL SEEKER ◆ He wants a parent, not a partner. He needs you "so much." In fact, he needs you to run his life for him. He has a difficult time doing adult things like working, completing chores, making decisions, being consistent, or paying his bills. He may give you lots of attention, but he will function very poorly in the real world.

THE EMOTIONALLY UNAVAILABLE MAN ❀ He is married, separated, engaged, dating someone else, or "just breaking up" with someone. He usually presents himself as "currently unhappy with" or "not quite out of" a relationship, but he is willing to have you on the side. Another type of emotionally unavailable man is the man who is preoccupied with his career, educational goals, hobbies, or other interests, to the exclusion of ever having a true interest in a long-term relationship. With the emotionally unavailable man, there is always a reason why he can't fully commit to you, but he's usually happy to keep stringing you along. After all, the situation is still convenient for him as long as you're willing to keep seeing him or sleeping with him on a "casual" basis despite the fact that he can't or won't get involved in a serious relationship with you.

THE MAN WITH THE HIDDEN LIFE ❀ He has undisclosed other lives that might include women, same-sex partners, children, jobs, wives, life-threatening addictions, criminal behavior, disease, or other histories that remain unrevealed to you for the long term or until you have been in the relationship a while and discover them yourself.

THE MENTALLY ILL MAN ❀ He can look normal on the outside, but after you've dated him for a while it becomes obvious that "something is amiss." Most women lack the training to know exactly what is wrong, but depending on his diagnosis he may be able to convince you to stay and "love him into wellness." He may hold you emotionally hostage by telling you that "everyone" leaves him, or by threatening self-harm if you leave.

THE ADDICT ❀ Many women do not recognize up front that he has an addiction, or they mistake it for his being a "fun-loving guy" who just wants to "party." Addictions can include sex, pornography, drugs, alcohol, thrill-seeking behaviors, gambling, food, or relationships. There are also what I call "pseudoproductive" addictions, which include addictions to work, perfection, outside approval, and achievements.

THE ABUSIVE OR VIOLENT MAN ◈ He starts out as very attentive and giving. But then Mr. Hyde appears—controlling, blaming, shaming, harming, perhaps hitting. Women who think abuse comes only in the form of a physical assault may miss warning signs of other kinds of abuse. Abuse can be verbal, emotional, spiritual, financial, physical, or sexual, or it can be abuse of the system to get his way. (Each of these is described in Chapter 9 of *How to Spot a Dangerous Man Before You Get Involved*.) With an abusive or violent man, anything goes when he decides he's in control, and he will always be in control. Abusive or violent behavior always gets worse over time.

THE EMOTIONAL PREDATOR ◈ He has a sixth sense about how women operate. He knows how to play to a woman's woundedness. Although his motives might be to prey on a woman's financial or sexual vulnerabilities (to name just a couple), he's called the "emotional" predator because he hunts for his victims by targeting their emotional vulnerabilities. He can sense women who have recently been dumped, or who are hurt, lonely, or sexually needy. He is a chameleon and can be whatever any woman needs him to be. He is very tuned in to a woman's body and eye language as well as to the subtle messages behind her words. He can pick up on hints about her life and turn himself into what she wants in the moment.

Many dangerous men fall into more than one category. I call these men *combo-pack men*. For instance, some addicts are also violent. Clingers and seekers almost always have interwoven mental-illness issues. Addicts are typically emotionally unavailable. Emotional predators usually have hidden lives, because hiding what they do is half the fun. Many combinations are possible, and some are fairly predictable.

Familiarize yourself with all eight categories even if you have not dated men from every category. You will want to have this knowledge for the future.

 # Mythical Assumptions

The mistakes made by women who get involved with dangerous men are based on myths. These women grew up believing false information taught to them and lived by their families, or they developed their own mythical beliefs about relationships by repeatedly dating dangerous men. Each go-round with a dangerous man teaches women falsehoods that they adopt as a part of their internal way of thinking about men and relationships. For more information about mythical assumptions and how women adopt them, review Chapters 2 and 12 of the main book.

This quiz will help you to uncover your own mythical assumptions about dangerous men. Mark each statement below as true or false:

_____ Dangerous men usually have professions that would seem obviously "dangerous" to an outsider, such as bodyguard. It is fairly easy to detect a dangerous man by his career.

_____ Dangerous men aren't firemen, social workers, teachers, or ministers.

_____ Dangerous men must come from dangerous families. You should be able to look at his family and tell if he is dangerous.

_____ Dangerous men look dangerous.

_____ Dangerous men do not look clean cut, handsome, conservative, or classy.

_____ A dangerous man will only come into my life once. If I've already dated one, I probably won't date another.

_____ Dangerous men have taught me well. If I was hurt by the previous one, I know I will see the next one coming.

_____ Dangerous men won't spend a lot of time getting to know me. If I have talked to a man for weeks by phone or in person but haven't yet dated him, he isn't a dangerous man.

_____ Dangerous men don't go to church, volunteer, help their mothers, or give to charities. If he is involved in community or religious activities, he isn't a dangerous man.

_____ Dangerous men don't disclose anything about themselves. This man has told me all about himself, so he couldn't be hiding anything.

All the above statements are false. Dangerous men do all the above _and more!_

# Universal Red Flags

Some red flags indicate undeniable truths. Women everywhere respond to these universal red flags when they're in the presence of a dangerous man. The wise woman will memorize, pay attention to, and utilize these signs as opportunities to reexamine the relationship—or to exit, if necessary. For more about red flags in general, review Chapter 2 of the main book. For lists of red flags for each category of dangerous man, review the sections titled "Red-Alert Behavioral Checklist" in Chapters 3 through 10.

Tell yourself the truth about your relationship. Take this quiz to see if any universal red flags are present in your current relationship. If you're not currently dating anyone, answer the questions as they relate to one or more of your past relationships, whether serious or casual.

Check all the following that apply, even if only remotely:

_____ You feel uncomfortable about something he has said or done, and the feeling remains.

_____ You often feel mad or scared, or he reminds you of someone else you know with a serious problem.

_____ You wish he would go away, you want to cry, you want to run away from him.

_____ You dread his phone calls.

_____ You are often bored with him.

_____ You think no one else in his life understands him.

_____ You think no one else in his life has ever really loved him/helped him.

_____ You think you are the only one who can help/love/understand him.

_____ You have the urge to "love him into emotional wellness," if that were possible.

_____ You think or wish you could help him "change" or "fix" his life.

_____ You let him borrow money from you or ask your friends to lend him money.

_____ You feel bad about yourself when you are around him.

_____ You only feel good about yourself when you are with him.

_____ You find your identity in your relationship with him.

_____ You feel he wants too much from you.

_____ You are emotionally tired from him; you feel he "sucks the life out of you."

_____ Your value system and his are very different, and it is problematic.

_____ Your past and his are very different, and the two of you have conflicts over it.

_____ You tell friends you are "unsure about the relationship."

_____ You feel isolated from other relationships with friends and family.

_____ You think he's too charming or a little "too good to be true."

_____ You feel in the wrong because he is always right and goes to great lengths to show you he is right.

_____ You are uncomfortable because he continually says he knows what is best for you.

_____ You notice he needs you too frequently, too much, or too intensely.

_____ You wonder if he really understands you or instead just claims to.

_____ You are uncomfortable because he has touched you inappropriately or too soon.

_____ You notice he quickly discloses information about his past or his emotional pain.

_____ You sense he is pushing too quickly for an emotional connection with you.

_____ He pushes you early on in the relationship to disclose information about your past.

_____ Although you don't believe it, he claims to feel an immediate connection with you (a sign of false intimacy).

_____ You see him pushing too quickly to get sexually involved with you, and you find yourself willing to abandon your sexual boundaries with him.

_____ You see him as a chameleon; you notice he can change to please whoever is in his presence.

_____ You notice how soon he tells you about his earlier failed relationships and about his previous partners and their flaws.

_____ You notice he mostly talks about himself, his plans, his future.

_____ You notice he spends a lot of time watching violent movies or TV or playing violent video games; he can be preoccupied with violence, death, or destruction.

_____ You have heard him confess to a current or previous drug addiction.

_____ You have information about major relationship problems that he handled poorly.

_____ He has confessed that he has been violent in the past or uses drugs or alcohol when stressed.

_____ You know he has multiple children by multiple partners, is inconsistent in paying child support, or rarely sees his children; you find yourself blaming the mother of his children for his behaviors.

_____ You find yourself accepting him "for now," even though you have plenty of red flags that would help you terminate the relationship if you paid attention to them.

_____ You find you would rather be entertained in this go-nowhere relationship than be bored alone.

_____ You make excuses for why you are dating him.

_____ You make excuses for his character and minimize his behavior.

_____ Your friends or family don't want to be around him.

_____ You make excuses and don't allow others to be around him because of what they think of him.

How many check marks do you have? _____

Is this relationship going in a direction that will fulfill your needs? Answer here:

_____

_____

_____

_____

_____

_____

# Family Traditions and Early Conditioning

Our family is part of the training ground that teaches us to either ignore or respect our red flags. We internalize our family's beliefs about women, men, relationships, boundaries, safety, verbalizing needs, or keeping quiet about unmet needs. These things are all taught to us by our families, yet the lessons are mostly unspoken.

Within families, women teach girls the same things that earlier generations of females were taught about men's behaviors, dating, marriage, and dangerousness in men. In some homes, women have normalized generations of negative behaviors by reframing or renaming them. They might say, "The Smith men always have tempers—it's the Irish in them," or, "The Schultz guys like their beer—it's in their blood," or, "The Brown men have a roving eye, but they always come home again." This kind of rationalizing trains young women to discount or ignore dangerous behaviors, minimize their unmet needs, and attempt to make relationships work at any cost. By internalizing these lessons, many women learn to consistently ignore their urgently waving red flags until they finally grow numb to them. For more about the role played by family conditioning in women's dating behavior, review Chapters 2 and 12 of the main book.

Did your family teach you any of the following, whether the lesson was spoken or unspoken? Mark all that apply.

Did you learn—

_____ to never say no to anything or anyone?

_____ to feel bad if you did say no?

_____ to rename men's problem behavior as something less threatening?

_____ to never give up on a failing relationship no matter what he has done?

_____ to remain forever optimistic that all men, no matter what their problems are, can change?

_____ to rescue unstable men from their own lives?

_____ to accept any kind of male attention and be glad to have it?

_____ to avoid speaking up when you feel you should because you're afraid doing so would bother him?

_____ to allow people to violate your boundaries without consequences?

_____ to violate your own values and morals by dating married men?

_____ to minimize dating married men?

_____ to not refuse a date simply because you are initially uncomfortable with a man?

_____ to resist labeling a man as alcoholic, mentally ill, problematic, or anything else that might make you reluctant to date him?

_____ to not expect people to earn your trust, but rather to trust them immediately?

_____ to expect addictions in men?

_____ to accept abusive behavior in men, whether it's verbal, emotional, physical, sexual, spiritual, or financial?

_____ to override your feelings of fear, concern, or discomfort with a man?

_____ to minimize a man's dangerous behavior?

_____ to normalize abnormal behavior that no one else would find normal?

_____ to avoid talking about these types of things with people outside the family?

Scoring

(Note: This is not a clinically verified scale.)

How many check marks do you have? _____

Under 5   Your relationship choices are affected by your family conditioning to only a small degree.

5–10   Probably half or less of your belief system about men and relationships has been tainted by your family conditioning. You are at moderate risk for choosing men based on this training. Consider seeing a counselor to work through this faulty framework of beliefs.

10–20   A large proportion of your belief system has been actively tainted by your family conditioning. You are at significant risk for choosing men based on these faulty beliefs. See a counselor immediately to address the toxic messages you internalized from your family of origin.

What did you notice from answering this questionnaire?

_____

_____

_____

_____

_____

_____

_____

_____

_____

How did it make you feel to realize these beliefs were a part of your family training?

_____

_____

_____

_____

_____

What, if anything, do you plan to do with the knowledge that your family conditioning has influenced your relationships with men?

_____

_____

_____

_____

_____

 # Loopholes

Women who are in dangerous relationships often must manipulate reality to justify staying in these go-nowhere relationships. Women who *repeatedly* get involved in dangerous relationships have an arsenal of "loopholes" they use in order to talk themselves into staying. These loopholes become a sort of "mantra" that women say to themselves over and over, either consciously or subconsciously. Loopholes reinforce women's decisions to stay with dangerous men, despite the red flags they have about their choices.

Some women have adopted these sabotaging loopholes based on what they think our culture expects of women in relationships. Others have learned them from women in their family who have taught them to accept dangerous behavior in men. Still others have created these loopholes for themselves.

If you want to change your patterns, it is important for you to know what kinds of loopholes you are using in order to avoid the change and growth required to end dangerous relationships. Below, place a check mark next to each of the loopholes you have used in any relationship. Later, when you are writing about your past experiences with dangerous men, you will have a chance to think more about your loopholes.

Loopholes Used to Minimize, or Downplay, Dangerous Behaviors

These loopholes make dangerous or unsatisfactory behaviors seem less threatening by minimizing their true effects. Phrases that represent this type of loophole often begin with the words "At least he...."

_____ At least he only drinks beer and not the hard stuff.

_____ At least he doesn't hit me; he only yells or threatens to.

_____ At least he works most of the time.

_____ At least he isn't like my dad/brother/previous boyfriend.

At least he _____

_____.

(fill in what you normally say)

≋ Loopholes Used to "Generalize" Dangerous Behaviors ≋

These loopholes reframe dangerous or unsatisfactory behaviors by making it seem as if *all* men engage in them, when in fact they do not. Phrases that represent this type of loophole often begin with the words "All (or most) men are like this...."

_____ All guys are like him, so why bother to end it?

_____ Boys will be boys.

_____ If I leave him I'll just end up with another one like him.

_____ All the good ones are taken.

_____ He's just like all the other men in my family.

All men _____

_____.

(fill in what you normally say)

≋ Loopholes Used to Justify Dangerous Behaviors ≋

These loopholes reframe dangerous or unsatisfactory behaviors in such a way that there seems to be a rational or short-term reason for staying and accepting them. Phrases that represent this type of loophole often begin with the words "I'm just staying because...."

_____ I'm just staying until someone better comes along.

_____ I'm just staying because he's helping me pay my bills, and he can stay until my bills are paid.

_____ I'm just staying because he's the father of my children, and I don't want my kids to be fatherless, no matter what.

_____ I'm just staying because I can't take care of myself/can't get out/have nowhere to go.

_____ I'm just staying because I don't want to be alone.

_____ I'm just staying because at least I know what to expect with him.

_____ I'm just staying because one day he will make something of himself.

_____ I'm just staying because at least he's someone to do things with.

I'm just staying because _____

_____.

(fill in what you normally say)

≋ *Wishful-Thinking Loopholes* ≋

These loopholes minimize the effects of dangerous or unsatisfactory behaviors because they allow you to believe he will change, when in fact he hasn't and probably won't. Minimizing his behaviors makes removing yourself from the relationship seem less urgent. Phrases that represent this type of loophole often begin with the words "He said he would...."

_____ He said he would get better/do better.

_____ He said we are going to try harder together.

_____ He said he would stop drinking/drugging/running around.

_____ He said he would go to church.

_____ He said he would marry me.

_____ He said he would not hit me/the kids again.

_____ He said he would get a job.

_____ He said he would pay more attention to me.

He said he would _____

_____ .

(fill in what you normally say)

≋ *Messiah-Complex Loopholes* ≋

These loopholes allow you to stay in a relationship because they allow you to operate under the fantasy that you have some magic power to change or improve him. Phrases that represent this type of loophole often begin with the words "No one else...."

_____ No one else knows him like I do.

_____ No one else has ever really understood him; that's all that's wrong.

_____ No one else has loved him like I do.

_____ No one else understands how much he needs me.

_____ No one else can help him get better the way I can.

_____ No one else besides me can keep him from drinking/drugging. If I stay in his life he will quit.

No one else _____

_____ .

(fill in what you normally say)

Extra-Credit Loopholes

These loopholes give him extra credit for accomplishing every-day adult responsibilities, when in fact what he is accomplishing are normal things that most adults should be doing anyway. Phrases that represent this type of loophole often begin with the words "He does..." or "He is...."

_____ He does buy diapers for the kids.

_____ He does go to work.

_____ He does come home every night.

_____ He does buy presents for the kids at Christmas.

_____ He does take the garbage out.

_____ He is handy/helpful around the house.

_____ He does nice things for me sometimes.

_____ He does drive me places.

_____ He does fun things with me sometimes.

He does/is _____

_____.

(fill in what you normally say)

Loopholes Used to Rename Dangerous Behaviors

These loopholes rename dangerous or unsatisfactory behaviors so they look less pathological. Phrases that represent this type of loophole often begin with the words "He needs..." or "He likes...."

_____ He likes his beer. (*The truth:* He drinks too much.)

_____ He needs a calm environment because he has a temper like his dad. (_The truth:_ He needs anger-management treatment.)

_____ He likes women because he's Italian and they have a roving eye. (_The truth:_ He runs around on me.)

_____ He needs quiet when he's home, so you just have to keep the kids quiet. (_The truth:_ He beats the kids when they are loud.)

_____ He likes to be noticed for working. (_The truth:_ He starts/stops employment when it suits him.)

_____ He likes his own opinions, and others don't always agree with him. (_The truth:_ He has problems getting along with others because he wants things his way.)

_____ He likes to get his way. (Or else...?)

He needs/likes _____

_____.

(fill in what you normally say)

≋ _Avoiding-the-Future Loopholes_ ≋

These loopholes allow you to think that dangerous or unsatisfactory behaviors are preferable to changing or being alone. Phrases that represent this type of loophole often begin with the words "I don't like..."

_____ I don't like doing things alone.

_____ I don't want to start over with someone else. I have five years in this relationship—I'll just make it work.

_____ I don't like the fact that I've already slept with him, but I since I have, I should try to make it work.

_____ I don't like dating and meeting people—I'd rather just stay with him.

_____ I don't like not knowing what to expect with new men—at least I know what to expect with him.

_____ I don't like the discomfort of new relationships. Our relationship is comfortable now.

_____ I don't like to turn a guy down, and it's looking like marriage, so it's too late to pull out now.

_____ I don't like the idea of starting over—my biological clock is ticking.

_____ I don't like the fact that all my girlfriends are married, which makes it so I don't have anyone else to do things with.

_____ I don't like going to parties as a single person—you're viewed as a threat, assuming you even get invited.

I don't like _____

_____.

(fill in what you normally say)

How many check marks do you have? _____

You will refer to this checklist when you're writing about your experiences with dangerous men.

Am I in Danger of Dating More Dangerous Men?

Since we cannot change reality, let us change the eyes which see reality.

— NIKOS KAZANTZAKIS

I've included this questionnaire in both the main book and the workbook because it's so important. If you haven't answered it yet, here's another chance to do so. If you have, it would be a good idea to either complete it again or to review your earlier answers now that you've done the other Part One exercises.

Give yourself two points for each "yes" answer, and zero points for each "no" answer.

_____ I have dated more than one dangerous man.

** _____ I have dated more than three dangerous men.

** _____ I have dated five or more dangerous men.

_____ I have broken up with and then gone back to a dangerous man.

** _____ A dangerous man I've dated would qualify as violent.

_____ A dangerous man I've dated would qualify as an addict.

_____ A dangerous man I've dated would qualify as mentally ill.

** _____ A dangerous man I've dated would qualify for any combination of violent, addicted, and mentally ill.

_____ I have a pattern of ignoring my red flags.

** _____ Ignoring my red flags has put me at risk with dangerous men.

_____ I don't even know what my red flags are.

_____ Friends and family are upset over the types of men I pick.

_____ I have dated emotionally unavailable men more than once.

_____ I don't know what healthy relationship patterns are.

_____ I fluctuate between men who are emotionally unavailable, have hidden lives, or are violent, and men who are permanent clingers or parental seekers.

_____ I don't fluctuate in the type of man I date; I keep picking the same type of dangerous man, even though it hasn't worked in the past.

_____ I grew up being taught to trust people unconditionally and to ignore my own feelings and intuition.

_____ **Total points**

The Dangerous-Man Risk Scale

(Note: This is not a clinically verified scale.) When considering your risk for dating dangerous men, in addition to adding up your points you must also consider *which* questions you answered yes to. Those marked with ** indicate higher risk; if you answered yes to *any* of these starred statements, that should raise additional concern.

0–8 points   Lower risk (unless you answered yes to any questions marked with **)

10–18 points   Moderate risk (unless you answered yes to any questions marked with **)

20–34 points   High risk (exceptionally high risk if you also answered yes to any questions marked with **)

Women who score in the moderate- and high-risk categories need to seek intervention on their own behalf. A first step toward doing so is completing this workbook, which can help you uncover, learn from, and change your self-sabotaging patterns. Beyond reading the main book and working through the workbook, you might also consider getting professional counseling to help you dismantle your destructive life patterns.

Your Notes: _____

_____

_____

_____

_____

_____

_____

_____

_____

_____

_____

_____

_____

_____

_____

PART TWO

Your Past Experiences with Dangerous Men

Identifying Feelings

Life itself remains a very effective therapist.

— KAREN H.

This page is for reference only. It contains a list of feeling words you can use as you write about your past experiences. If you need help exploring and labeling the feelings associated with past experiences, use the following list to prompt you:

accepted	disappointed	secure	sad
afraid	embarrassed	insecure	independent
angry	envious	jealous	shameful
attractive	frustrated	judged	shy
beaten down	excited	lonely	silly
brave	fearful	loser	stupid
calm	friendless	loyal	superior
cheated	grateful	worthless	ugly
cheerful	guilty	macho	unaccepted
confused	happy	needy	unappreciated
contempt	hate	neglected	used
courageous	helpless	persecuted	useless
cowardly	hopeless	phony	violent
cruel	hurt	proud	misunderstood
defeated	hypocritical	regretful	_____
degraded	ignored	rejected	_____
desperate	impatient	repulsive	_____

# My First Dangerous-Man Experience

Truth is the only safe ground to stand upon.

— Elizabeth Cady Stanton

In this exercise you are asked to look at the facts behind your first relationship with a dangerous man: how old you were, the length of the relationship, how you met him, and the actual story of your relationship. This is what writers call the "narrative arc." Answering these questions for all the dangerous men you've been involved with will give you an opportunity to see how the relationships were similar to or different from one another.

If necessary, remember to make extra copies of the next three exercises so you have a blank set for each dangerous relationship you've been involved in.

His name: _____ How old were you?_____

How many men in total had you dated before him? _____

How long did you date him? _____

How did you meet? _____

_____

_____

_____

_____

_____

Tell the rest of your relationship story with this dangerous man. Include descriptions of what made him dangerous. (To help you with this part of the question, you may want to review Chapters 3 through 10 of the main book.)

_____

_____

_____

_____

_____

_____

_____

_____

_____

_____

_____

_____

_____

_____

_____

_____

_____

_____

_____

_____

≋ *My Patterns with My First Dangerous Man* ≋

Anything of value is going to cost you something.

— Toni Cade Bambara

This section walks you through a review of the specifics about how you met this dangerous man, characteristics he may have had that were similar to those of other people in your life, and healthy and unhealthy patterns in the relationship. As you answer these questions for each relationship you've had with a dangerous man, you can begin to see patterns in how you've related to men up to now.

Is the manner in which you met your first dangerous man a healthy or unhealthy way of meeting men?

Why?

_____

_____

_____

Did your first dangerous man have characteristics that were like those of someone else you know currently or knew in the past? If so, who?

_____

How was your first dangerous man like this person?

_____

_____

_____

_____

35

Does your first dangerous man have any similarities to your father or to any other man who raised you or was influential in your childhood?

_____

If so, what similarities?

_____

_____

Have you previously dated or married anyone who had characteristics similar to those of your father or another influential man from your childhood?

_____

If so, who?

_____

How did that relationship work out in terms of those characteristics?

_____

_____

_____

What was the early part of your relationship like with your first dangerous man? What parts were healthy?

_____

_____

_____

_____

_____

What parts were unhealthy?

_____

_____

_____

_____

_____

What should you have paid more attention to in the beginning of the relationship?

_____

_____

_____

_____

_____

_____

_____

What could you have done differently in terms of the circumstances under which you met him that would have protected you more effectively?

_____

_____

_____

_____

_____

_____

_____

≋ *My Red Flags with My First Dangerous Man* ≋

What you risk reveals what you value.

— JEANNETTE WINTERSON

This section is very important because it will help you to gain insight. Here you will be asked to tune in to the physiological, emotional, and sexual reactions you had to each dangerous man you've been involved with. You will be asked to notice responses you had to him that seemed familiar to you and thus might have made being with him comfortable for you, early childhood messages you may have received about trusting people unconditionally, and the specific red flags you ignored when you got involved with him. Becoming aware of exactly what you believed and ignored each time you got involved with a dangerous man is crucial to helping you recognize red flags the next time around.

I noticed a physical reaction to this man because of what I felt in my body. This reaction was a sensation of:

_____

_____

_____

_____

I noticed a mental reaction to this man because of what I felt emotionally. This emotional reaction was:

_____

_____

_____

_____

I felt a sexual reaction to this man. It felt like:

_____

_____

_____

_____

I noticed a familiarity with this man because he reconnected me to the memory of:

_____

_____

_____

This man reminded me of another person in my life who was (describe the similarities be-tween the two individuals):

_____

_____

The person he reminded me of was a negative or positive influence in my life (choose one or both):

_____

_____

How?

_____

_____

_____

_____

Could this person and their influence in my life have contributed to why I selected this particular dangerous man?

_____

Why?

_____

_____

_____

_____

_____

While growing up I received the following messages from my parents about "trusting" other people:

_____

_____

_____

_____

_____

As a child did I receive the message that I should unconditionally trust people? Or, instead, did I receive the message that people needed to prove themselves? Explain:

_____

_____

_____

_____

_____

How can making people "prove themselves" benefit me when it comes to relationships?

_____

_____

_____

_____

Can I change my habits of trusting people unconditionally, especially if they have proven themselves to be unreliable and untrustworthy? Will doing so mean letting go of some of my childhood conditioning or training? Explain:

_____

_____

_____

_____

How can I do this?

_____

_____

_____

_____

From the checklists I marked in the section on loopholes, what loopholes did I use in this particular dangerous relationship to justify staying?

_____

_____

_____

_____

What other loopholes did I use in this relationship that were not included on the checklist?

_____

_____

_____

_____

Do any of the loopholes sound familiar—like I learned them in my family or from cultural messages? Where did I learn them?

_____

_____

_____

_____

I remember my first red flag with this man as:

_____

_____

_____

_____

I ignored it because:

_____

_____

_____

_____

Other red flags I had were:

_____

_____

_____

_____

I continued to ignore them because:

_____

_____

_____

_____

The eventual consequences for me that stemmed from ignoring the red flags in this relationship were:

_____

_____

_____

_____

The first red flag I had with this man and the reason the relationship did not work may have been related. If so, how?

_____

_____

_____

_____

Here's what I learned from these red flags:

_____

_____

_____

_____

_____

_____

_____

My Second
Dangerous-Man Experience

His name: _____ How old were you? _____

How many men in total had you dated before him? _____

How long did you date him? _____

How did you meet? _____

_____

_____

_____

_____

_____

Tell the rest of your relationship story with this dangerous man. Include descriptions of what made him dangerous. (To help you with this part of the question, you may want to review Chapters 3 through 10 of the main book.)

_____

_____

_____

_____

_____

_____

_____

_____

_____

_____

_____

_____

_____

_____

_____

_____

≋ _My Patterns with My Second Dangerous Man_ ≋

Is the manner in which you met your second dangerous man a healthy or unhealthy way of meeting men?

Why?

_____

_____

_____

_____

_____

Did your second dangerous man have characteristics that were like those of someone else you know currently or knew in the past? If so, who?

_____

_____

How was your second dangerous man like this person?

_____

_____

_____

_____

Does your second dangerous man have any similarities to your father or to any other man who raised you or was influential in your childhood?

_____

If so, what similarities?

_____

_____

_____

_____

Have you previously dated or married anyone who had characteristics similar to those of your father or another influential man from your childhood?

_____

If so, who?

_____

How did that relationship work out in terms of those characteristics?

_____

_____

_____

_____

What was the early part of your relationship like with your second dangerous man? What parts were healthy?

_____

_____

_____

_____

What parts were unhealthy?

_____

_____

_____

_____

What should you have paid more attention to in the beginning of the relationship?

_____

_____

_____

_____

What could you have done differently in terms of the circumstances under which you met him that would have protected you more effectively?

_____

_____

_____

_____

_____

≋ *My Red Flags with My Second Dangerous Man* ≋

I noticed a physical reaction to this man because of what I felt in my body. This reaction was a sensation of:

_____

_____

_____

I noticed a mental reaction to this man because of what I felt emotionally. This emotional reaction was:

_____

_____

_____

_____

I felt a sexual reaction to this man. It felt like:

_____

_____

_____

I noticed a familiarity with this man because he reconnected me to the memory of:

_____

_____

_____

This man reminded me of another person in my life who was (describe the similarities between the two individuals):

_____

_____

_____

The person he reminded me of was a negative or positive influence in my life (choose one or both):

_____

_____

How?

_____

_____

_____

_____

Could this person and their influence in my life have contributed to why I selected this particular dangerous man?

_____

Why?

_____

_____

_____

_____

_____

From the checklists I marked in the section on loopholes, what loopholes did I use in this particular dangerous relationship to justify staying?

_____

_____

_____

_____

What other loopholes did I use in this relationship that were not included on the checklist?

_____

_____

_____

_____

Do any of the loopholes sound familiar—like I learned them in my family or from cultural messages? Where did I learn them?

_____

_____

_____

51

Were my loopholes with this man similar to any of the ones I used in earlier relationships with dangerous men?

_____

How are they the same or different?

_____

_____

_____

_____

Why?

_____

_____

_____

_____

_____

I remember my first red flag with this man as:

_____

_____

_____

I ignored it because:

_____

_____

_____

_____

Other red flags I had were:

_____

_____

_____

_____

I continued to ignore them because:

_____

_____

_____

_____

The eventual consequences for me that stemmed from ignoring the red flags in this relationship were:

_____

_____

_____

_____

The first red flag I had with this man and the reason the relationship did not work may have been related. If so, how?

_____

_____

_____

_____

Here's what I learned from these red flags:

_____

_____

_____

_____

_____

_____

My Third
Dangerous-Man Experience

His name: _____ How old were you? _____

How many men in total had you dated before him? _____

How long did you date him? _____

How did you meet? _____

_____

_____

_____

_____

_____

Tell the rest of your relationship story with this dangerous man. Include descriptions of what made him dangerous. (To help you with this part of the question, you may want to review Chapters 3 through 10 of the main book.)

_____

_____

_____

_____

_____

_____

_____

_____

_____

_____

_____

_____

_____

_____

_____

_____

≋ *My Patterns with My Third Dangerous Man* ≋

Is the manner in which you met your third dangerous man a healthy or unhealthy way of meeting men?

Why?

_____

_____

_____

_____

Did your third dangerous man have characteristics that were like those of someone else you know currently or knew in the past? If so, who?

_____

How was your third dangerous man like this person?

_____

_____

_____

_____

Does your third dangerous man have any similarities to your father or to any other man who raised you or was influential in your childhood?

_____

If so, what similarities?

_____

_____

_____

_____

Have you previously dated or married anyone who had characteristics similar to those of your father or another influential man from your childhood?

_____

If so, who?

_____

How did that relationship work out in terms of those characteristics?

_____

_____

_____

_____

What was the early part of your relationship like with your third dangerous man? What parts were healthy?

_____

_____

_____

_____

What parts were unhealthy?

_____

_____

_____

_____

What should you have paid more attention to in the beginning of the relationship?

_____

_____

_____

_____

What could you have done differently in terms of the circumstances under which you met him that would have protected you more effectively?

_____

_____

_____

_____

_____

≋ *My Red Flags with My Third Dangerous Man* ≋

I noticed a physical reaction to this man because of what I felt in my body. This reaction was a sensation of:

_____

_____

_____

I noticed a mental reaction to this man because of what I felt emotionally. This emotional reaction was:

_____

_____

_____

I felt a sexual reaction to this man. It felt like:

_____

_____

_____

I noticed a familiarity with this man because he reconnected me to the memory of:

_____

_____

This man reminded me of another person in my life who was (describe the similarities between the two individuals):

_____

_____

_____

_____

The person he reminded me of was a negative or positive influence in my life (choose one or both):

_____

_____

How?

_____

_____

_____

_____

_____

Could this person and their influence in my life have contributed to why I selected this particular dangerous man?

_____

Why?

_____

_____

_____

From the checklists I marked in the section on loopholes, what loopholes did I use in this particular dangerous relationship to justify staying?

_____

_____

_____

_____

What other loopholes did I use in this relationship that were not included on the checklist?

_____

_____

_____

Do any of the loopholes sound familiar—like I learned them in my family or from cultural messages? Where did I learn them?

_____

_____

_____

Were my loopholes with this man similar to any of the ones I used in earlier relationships with dangerous men?

_____

How are they the same or different?

_____

_____

_____

_____

Why?

_____

_____

_____

I remember my first red flag with this man as:

_____

_____

I ignored it because:

_____

_____

_____

_____

Other red flags I had were:

_____

_____

_____

I continued to ignore them because:

_____

_____

_____

The eventual consequences for me that stemmed from ignoring the red flags in this relation-ship were:

_____

_____

_____

The first red flag I had with this man and the reason the relationship did not work may have been related. If so, how?

_____

_____

_____

Here's what I learned from these red flags:

_____

_____

_____

_____

_____

_____

_____

_____

# Part Two Summary

And the day came when the risk it took to remain tight in the bud was more painful than the risk it took to blossom.

— ANAIS NIN

You have just done some great, insightful work on examining your relationship patterns! Completing the exercises in Part Two has provided you with the opportunity to look deeply at your relationship history, and you have gathered very important and lifesaving information from answering these questions. Your responses hold key information about patterns in your involvement with dangerous men. The types of dangerous men you've been drawn to, their characteristics that felt familiar, and what in your background contributed to your choosing these men are all spelled out in these pages. Together, your answers form a sort of "composite" of the types of dangerous men you have chosen in the past. Furthermore, you can now see *how* those relationships happened by examining the red flags you missed or ignored. The fact that your red flags proved accurate should demonstrate to you that you can trust them in the future. From this moment forward, paying attention to your red flags can help you to change your selection patterns. But for them to work you must heed their lifesaving messages.

You are now a step closer to applying the lessons from your past relationships toward building a healthier future. In Part Three you will put together the big picture.

PART THREE

Making New Choices

Introduction to Part Three

Be the change you want to see in the world.

— MAHATMA GANDHI

Naïveté is not a life skill. But putting knowledge to practical use is! And you have gained immense knowledge from completing the exercises in this workbook so far. You have laid the groundwork for examining the life lessons you've learned from your relationship history. Part Three will help you to take an in-depth, clear-eyed look at those lessons, and it will help you to use that knowledge to create new possibilities for your future.

Every relationship offers a unique set of lessons. Part Three starts by asking you to look at what each dangerous relationship taught you. It is crucial that women become aware of what they learned from their past relationships so they can hone their critical-thinking skills and put them to proper use when considering future relationships. This big-picture thinking involves stepping back, looking at the facts, identifying patterns from your history, comparing and contrasting past relationships, gauging your responses to a potential new dating partner, and developing a plan for avoiding past destructive behaviors.

This examination of lessons learned will prepare you to do the second exercise, in which you will list the specific characteristics that qualify each of your past dangerous men as dangerous. From those lists you will create a personalized do-not-date list, a tool for helping you to see overlapping traits in men that you have consistently been attracted to and yet have missed identifying as dangerous. Your do-not-date list is essentially a contract with yourself to avoid certain characteristics in the men you date. Creating the list is a concrete step toward using your new knowledge to build skills for preventing dangerous relationships in the future.

Finally, the last exercise asks you to examine your present relationship, using the knowledge you've gained from working through the workbook. (If you're not currently in a relationship, keep the questionnaire to use the next time you do get involved with someone.) It asks you to develop a detailed plan for what you will do if you discover characteristics in your new man that match some of those on your do-not-date list, and it asks you to discuss your plan with your accountability partner.

This part of the workbook aims to help you claim your reward for digging deeply into your past relationships: the ability to make better decisions so you can choose healthier relationships. Your soul-searching and insight will pay off as you build a future bright with new possibilities!

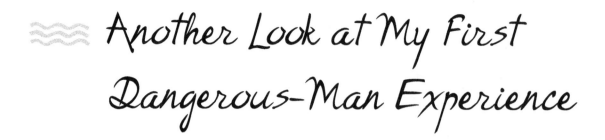

Another Look at My First Dangerous-Man Experience

≈≈≈ *What I Learned from My First Dangerous Man* ≈≈≈

One of the marks of a gift is to have the courage of it.

— KATHERINE ANNE PORTER

This exercise asks you to examine what worked in your past dangerous relationships, what didn't work, and what you will do differently in the future. When answering these questions, take the time to think through how to make a different choice next time.

If necessary, remember to make extra copies of this exercise and the next one so you have a blank set for each dangerous relationship you've been involved in.

What didn't work in the relationship with my first dangerous man?

_____

_____

_____

_____

_____

_____

_____

Why?

_____

_____

_____

_____

What scared me about the man, the relationship, and my choices?

_____

_____

_____

_____

What did I learn about these characteristics in men?

_____

_____

_____

_____

What did I learn about myself from choosing this dangerous man?

_____

_____

_____

_____

What will I do differently now?

_____

_____

_____

_____

_____

_____

_____

_____

≋ My Do-Not-Date List of Characteristics ≋ from My First Dangerous Man

Freedom is always freedom for the one who thinks differently.

— ROSA LUXEMBERG

Complete the list below by writing in specific words describing the characteristics that cause you to realize this man was dangerous. Use adjectives like "disrespectful," "irresponsible," "controlling," "married," "alcoholic," "verbally abusive," "violent"—whatever applies. What you are doing is listing traits you can later recognize in other men who may be dangerous. This exercise allows you to condense all your insights and experiences into one specific list of characteristics that you can flag in your mind as "dangerous."

❑ ❑ ❑

The characteristics of _____ (his name)
that made me realize he was a dangerous man:

_____   Comments: _____

_____   _____

_____   _____

_____   _____

_____   _____

_____   _____

_____   _____

_____   _____

This dangerous man primarily fits into which category(ies)? List all that apply. (Review "Categories of Dangerous Men," in Part One.)

_____

_____

_____

_____

_____

_____

_____

_____

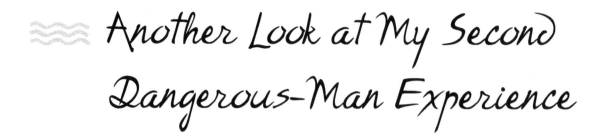

Another Look at My Second Dangerous-Man Experience

≋ What I Learned from My Second Dangerous Man ≋

What didn't work in the relationship with my second dangerous man?

_____

_____

_____

_____

Why?

_____

_____

_____

_____

What scared me about the man, the relationship, and my choices?

_____

_____

_____

_____

What did I learn about these characteristics in men?

_____

_____

_____

_____

_____

What did I learn about myself from choosing this dangerous man?

_____

_____

_____

_____

_____

What will I do differently now?

_____

_____

_____

_____

_____

_____

≋ *My Do-Not-Date List of Characteristics* ≋
from My Second Dangerous Man

The characteristics of _____ (his name)
that made me realize he was a dangerous man:

_____   Comments: _____

_____   _____

_____   _____

_____   _____

_____   _____

_____   _____

_____   _____

This dangerous man primarily fits into which category(ies)? List all that apply. (Review "Categories of Dangerous Men," in Part One.)

_____

_____

_____

_____

_____

_____

_____

_____

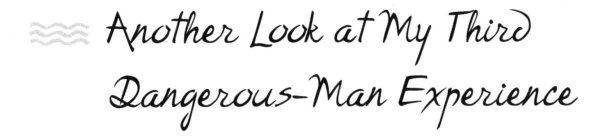# Another Look at My Third Dangerous-Man Experience

≋ *What I Learned from My Third Dangerous Man* ≋

What didn't work in the relationship with my third dangerous man?

_____

_____

_____

_____

Why?

_____

_____

_____

_____

What scared me about the man, the relationship, and my choices?

_____

_____

_____

_____

What did I learn about these characteristics in men?

_____

_____

_____

_____

_____

_____

What did I learn about myself from choosing this dangerous man?

_____

_____

_____

_____

_____

_____

_____

What will I do differently now?

_____

_____

_____

_____

_____

_____

≋ *My Do-Not-Date List of Characteristics* ≋
from My Third Dangerous Man

The characteristics of _____ (his name)
that made me realize he was a dangerous man:

_____   Comments: _____

_____   _____

_____   _____

_____   _____

_____   _____

_____   _____

_____   _____

This dangerous man primarily fits into which category(ies)? List all that apply. (Review "Categories of Dangerous Men," in Part One.)

_____

_____

_____

_____

_____

_____

_____

# My Personalized Do-Not-Date List

"Integrity is doing the right thing, even if nobody is watching."

— JIM STOVALL

Go back through this part of the workbook to the do-not-date lists from each of the dangerous men you've been involved with. Below, write down every characteristic from each of the lists. What you are doing is combining all the lists into one long list, which will help you to see all of the traits on one page. If a characteristic appears in more than one list, write it just once in this new list, but place an asterisk beside it for each list it appears in. Traits marked with asterisks indicate special red flags for you, because they show that you have a pattern of getting involved with men who have this particular dangerous trait.

When you are finished, you will have a profile of the kinds of dangerous men you have dated in the past and that you will *not* want to date in the future. The list you are creating is a compilation of the red flags and warnings you've previously ignored. Since you have advance knowledge of these red flags and warnings, you have the opportunity to utilize them to keep yourself safe. Any time you begin dating a new man, refer back to this page to see if any of his characteristics match your old, unhealthy dating patterns. In addition, ask your family and friends if they see anything in the new man that makes them think you should refresh your memory by reviewing this list.

Here is my personalized do-not-date list of characteristics, based on my experiences with dangerous men:

_____   _____

_____   _____

_____   _____

_____   _____

_____   _____

_____   _____

_____   _____

_____   _____

_____   _____

_____   _____

_____   _____

Red Flags and Patterns in My New Relationships

The best time to see the light is as soon as you can.

— TONI R.

Use this questionnaire to write about your current dating experiences. It asks you to focus on what you are doing, what your red flags are telling you, how the relationship is similar to or different from previous ones, and what you will do in the face of what you discover about your present dating experience. If you're not currently involved with anyone, keep this questionnaire handy so you can work through it the next time you consider dating someone.

Name of new man: _____

How this relationship is *like* any previous negative relationship(s):

_____

_____

_____

How this relationship is *not like* previous negative relationship(s):

_____

_____

_____

What I will watch for in this relationship:

_____

_____

_____

Red flags I have noticed:

_____

_____

What I plan to do about the red flags right now:

_____

_____

_____

Here's my specific plan for *what* I will do and *when* I will do it if the relationship turns bad (write out a step-by-step plan that includes talking with others, gauging the message of your red flag, how you will verify what your red flag is trying to tell you, *what* you will do if the red flag turns out to be true, and *when* you will do it):

_____

_____

_____

_____

_____

_____

_____

_____

_____

_____

_____

_____

_____

_____

_____

_____

_____

_____

I have shared this information with my accountability partner, and here is her response:

_____

_____

_____

_____

# Part Three Summary

Knowledge speaks, but wisdom listens.

— JIMI HENDRIX

Congratulations! You have completed an insight-oriented process of gathering critical information about who you have been with and what you have learned. This information has the potential to open new doors for you now that you are clear about the dangerous traits you have been drawn to in the past and the kinds of men you will not date in the future.

How else can you reap the most benefits from this information? As I discussed in the Introduction, one of the most constructive things you can do is develop an accountability program with another woman or other women who have the same goals. Being accountable to others keeps women honest about their thinking, about their slipups, and about their overall recovery goals. Knowing that you have to answer for your behavior to a safe and trusted other can help to keep you on track. And developing a support system that includes getting tips from other women about how to stay on track is the backbone of any healthy recovery program. Additionally, having a support system prevents isolation, which is a setup for relapse. Hooking up with other women who are committed to healthier relationships is a win-win for all involved.

It is also crucial to develop a *written* plan for what you will do in future relationships if your red flags begin waving wildly. That's why I allowed plenty of space for the answer to that question in the last exercise. Simply thinking, "I will deal with that if it happens" is not a plan. It's a loophole. A woman's ability to exit a relationship quickly and safely is far more important than her ability to attract dates. Having a "pre-plan" in place keeps you on the lookout in every relationship.

Lastly, the information you've gained and the insight you've developed from working through this program must be seen as part of a larger lifestyle change. This is not just information for today; it is information for forever. If you ever stop using the information, you will place yourself at the same level of risk for getting involved with dangerous men as you were before. This is not a "dating diet" that calls for you to change a few patterns for the short term. This is a long-term view of relationships and of dangerousness that must become part of your overall lifestyle.

 # in Closing

Things do not change, we change.

— HENRY DAVID THOREAU

Consistently living by the information and processes provided in the *How to Spot a Dangerous Man* book and workbook will help you to reduce your exposure and vulnerability to dangerous men. It is my hope that you have taken to heart the information provided in this curriculum about the incurability of pathology, the importance of listening to your red flags, the categories and behaviors of dangerous men, and your own selection patterns. It is my hope that you have made the decision to honor your do-not-date list.

Just as important, it is also my hope that you will share this message with other women. We live in a world where women's politeness is more valued than their safety. Some of us grew up in homes where our female elders trained us to accept and rename dangerous behaviors in men. These messages to women and girls need to change. This is the generation that needs to teach the next one the truth about dangerous relationships. New and healthier approaches to relationships need to become the norm. All women need to know about pathology and red flags. Information about the types of dangerous men and how they operate should be given to girls as early as middle school. And reflecting on one's own selection patterns should be something a woman automatically learns to do.

For all this to happen, women need to teach women. Be the light to other women. Pass it forward.

Thank you for learning and growing.

Resources

For detailed information on the topics addressed in this work-book, see *How to Spot a Dangerous Man Before You Get Involved* (Hunter House, 2005).

≈≈ *Author Contact / Website / Workshops* ≈≈

Sandra L. Brown, M.A.
Website: www.saferelationships.com

Sandra offers workshops, lectures, and retreats on the topic of dangerous men and other topics related to self-help, mental health, and relationships. Contact the author to develop a work-shop for your group.

The author's website provides information on upcoming workshops, tips for spotting dangerous men, a resource for or-dering books and workbooks, and information about the author's upcoming books. Other features include Once upon a Time (women can submit stories about their involvement with dangerous men); Dangerous Man Quizzes (are you at risk?); a Q & A with the author about dangerous relationships; Share & Care (women share their red flags); Doc on the Clock (have a counseling session with Sandra and bill your credit card); and reviews of *How to Spot a Dangerous Man Before You Get Involved* and other, related books.

To have an e-zine delivered to your e-mail address, please send an e-mail to the author at the address listed above. Your e-mail address and other contact information will *never* be shared with anyone.

Resources for Women in Abusive Relationships

www.ncadv.org ◆ **National Coalition Against Domestic Violence.** Call toll free (800) 799-SAFE (7233). This organization maintains a data bank of domestic-violence shelters in communities all across the country. It can refer you to one located close to where you live.

www.nsvrc.org ◆ **National Sexual Violence Research Center.** This website lists locations and phone numbers of state and territory coalitions.

www.ncvc.org ◆ **National Center for Victims of Crime.** A website full of information on various types of crime that also includes national resources and contacts.

www.ndvh.org ◆ **National Domestic Violence Hotline.** A national data bank for referrals to local resources.

www.womenslawproject.org ◆ **The Women's Law Project.** A national organization devoted to legal issues relating to women.

Any sheriff department, police department, social service office, victim advocate, or shelter can help you find the necessary local resources to obtain the support and assistance you need to get out of a dangerous relationship, but you must reach out. Call one of these professionals today.

≋ *Other Websites* ≋

Information

www.Mentalhealth.com ◆ An encyclopedia describing mental illnesses, treatments, and medications.

www.Hare.org ◆ Lists books on psychopathology and features the Hare checklist of psychopathology symptoms.

www.Crisiscounseling.com ◆ Click on "Problems and Disorders," where you will find a variety of explanations regarding various mental-health issues, including signs of psychopathology.

www.Oregoncounseling.org ◈ Various useful articles on cyber-addiction, stalking, and psychopaths.

www.Geometry.net ◈ Research bank offering descriptions of many psychological disorders, including personality disorders.

www.QuestionsBeforeMarriage.net ◈ Good dating information. Click on "Dangerous Mates" to see a list of red-flag behaviors.

www.CrimeLibrary.com ◈ Interesting, true stories about some of society's most infamous psychopaths.

www.ama-assn.org ◈ Information on violence prevention from the American Medical Association.

www.end-harassment.com ◈ Harassment hotline: Information and resources for victims of stalking and sexual harassment.

www.rosefund.org ◈ ROSE stands for "regaining one's self-esteem." Assistance with rebuilding your life after violence.

www.vaw.umn.edu ◈ Violence Against Women's online resources. Law, advocacy, and social services.

www.nicp.net ◈ U.S. National Crime Prevention website.

www.justicewomen.com ◈ Website for Women's Justice Center, which is part of the U.S. Department of Justice.

www.groups.msn.com/narcissisticpersonalitydisorder/home1. msnw ◈ Website on narcissism as a mental-health problem.

www.groups.msn.com/psychopath/home.htm ◈ Website on psychopathology.

Services

www.serenityfound.org ◈ Twelve-step organization.

www.TrustMeID.com ◈ Self-identification background checks. You can run a background check about yourself, then allow others to see it as verification of what you are claiming about yourself and your history.

www.Verifiedperson.com Background searches that include nationwide criminal history, sex offender status, age, identity, city of residence, living status, marital status, children in the household, work history, educational history, professional licenses, professional references, and U.S. employment eligibility.

www.Peopledata.com Background searches and satellite photo services.

www.Rapsheets.com Criminal background checks.

www.Datesmart.com Private investigation services into any area of a person's background.

www.Entersect.net Identify online validation systems that search court records, civil histories (e.g., marriages and divorces), addresses, etc.

Printed in the USA
CPSIA information can be obtained
at www.ICGtesting.com
JSHW060048150824
68134JS00031B/2667

9 780897 934527